First English edition published by
Editions Minerva S.A., Genève
Copyright © MCMLXXVI by Editions Minerva S.A., Genève and
Copyright © MCMLXXX by Productions Liber S.A., Fribourg
All rights reserved
ISBN: 0-517-314592
This edition is published by Crescent Books,
a division of Crown Publishers, Inc.
a b c d e f g h
Printed in Italy

PARIS

Text by

Pierre Leprohon

Translated by Blanche Michaels

Crescent Books
NEW YORK

One can speak of the grandeur of Rome, the picturesqueness of Amsterdam, the austerity of London, the warmth of Madrid, the poetry of Leningrad, but for Paris one must reserve the word "charm" and this is the way the visitor to Paris defines its attraction. Undoubtedly, he is more susceptible to its charm than the Parisian who lives there, and though the years go by and the centuries pass, that charm remains, as does the beauty of a soul after the loveliness of a face has faded.

Paris has been sung by poets, coveted by princes and chosen by the proscribed. A Paris of two thousand years spent on the banks of a river that lingers as it flows, to listen to voices of the past and mirror the shadows of the dead, a Paris constantly ravaged, yet always living on, a Paris so often pillaged, yet endlessly reborn. Two thousand years have made it what it is today with its scars and its voids, its memories and its treasures. This is a city with an overt and, at the same time, a covert face. The stranger may think he has solved its riddle, but he must be prepared to dig deep without much hope of final success.

The Parisian sky, sometimes clear but often gray, has been praised. Its light is its soul — soft to the gaze, it could be called discreet, sensitive and variable — changing at the will of the seasons and the hours. This light glides over things without destroying them, just right to mould a wall or turn blue the angle of a roof. And even more than this light, there floats that imponderable called "the air of Paris".

The air of Paris! It is also in a woman's smile, in the color of a stone, and in a child's game. It is in the song on the lips of a working girl, in the eyes of an exile.

We must blame the harshness of the times if the rhythm of modern life — and it is as demanding here as elsewhere — has made the Parisian less charming than his reputation claims and the crowd lose something of its cordiality and its joy. The tenderness is still there, beneath the banter and caprice.

Besides, every city has a hundred faces — and Paris more than any other. The traveler who would limit his knowledge to only some of these faces would be a bad judge of Paris. Luxury and elegance, work and business, memories of Old Paris and nights of Gay Paris, these are the facets of this kaleidoscope where each one can find what he seeks. However, he should beware of trusting too much to appearances, of mistaking negligence for indiscipline, irony for vanity, insouciance for poverty. That is the way it is with the "hobos", those "hippies" of another age who prefer to lie on benches on the square or underneath bridges rather than enjoy the benefits of the social order and who the surprised tourist can still see sleeping soundly on the Metro's heating grilles.

From the Champs-Elysées — not always the "residence of the gods", or even of the financiers! — to

Right: various views of the cathedral of Notre Dame and the nearby quays on the Seine.

4

Charonne or Belleville, people of all social classes, all ages, all ethnic groups from other continents live side by side without ever getting to know each other very well. Paris is made up of this multitude. With the satellite cities that encircle the capital, "Greater Paris" today groups a sixth of the French population. So, by getting to know Paris you will also be getting to know a good many of the French.

Cities come into the world like fruit, from a seed which is the germ and the substance. They develop like sapwood in concentric waves.

We have seen that Paris grew in this way, extending its boundaries through the centuries. By going back to the beginning of the ages, one finds the heart of the city.

Twin islands, forming a single mass, have for thousands of years watched the waters of the Seine River flow past. The waters are the embryo from which life has sprung and the city has prospered.

And so it is fitting that we should first turn our attention to the Ile de la Cité. If the traveler had wings, he would see from the air what the imagination

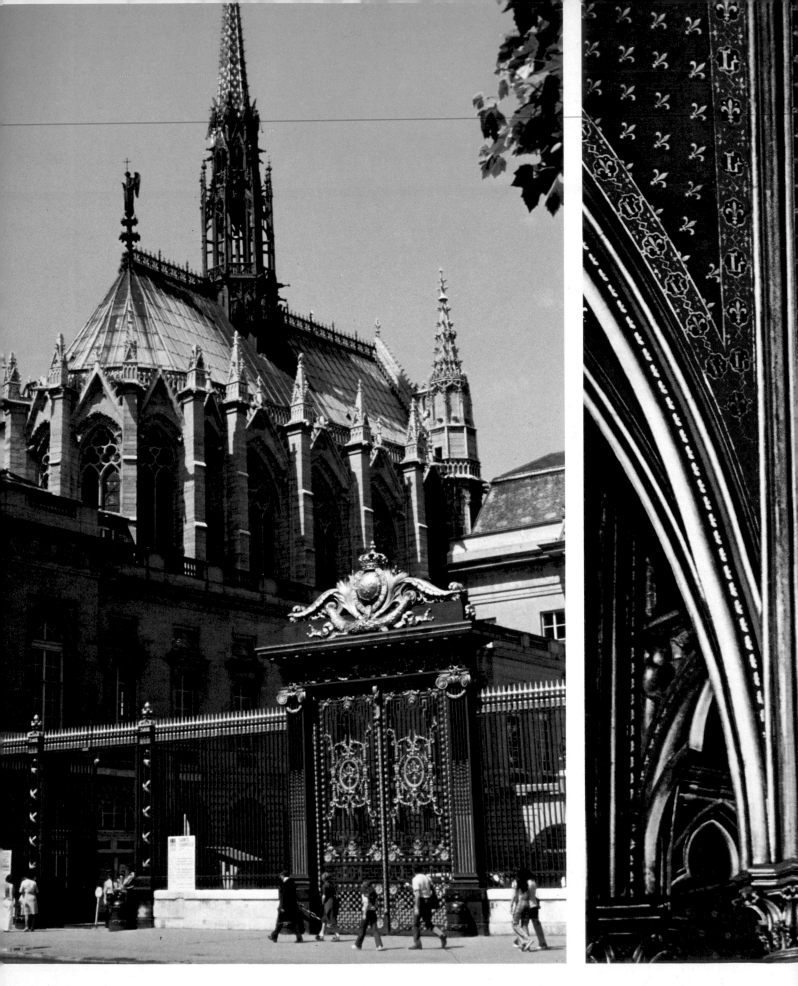

Left: the Sainte-Chapelle, in the heart of Ile de la Cité. Next to the church, the wrought-iron gates of the Palais de Justice.

Center: detail of the vaults of the Sainte-Chapelle.

Like those of Notre Dame, the stained glass windows of the Sainte-Chapelle are among the most beautiful to be found in any church in Paris. Above: one of the windows.

of the poets Hugo and D'Annunzio has already revealed: a ship whose prow tapers to the tip of the Vert-Galant and whose poop is outlined at Pont Sully. A ship of stone, set between the waters and the greenery, its main mast the towers of Notre-Dame. Solidly moored by a dozen bridges, the ship of Paris has as its motto—which is also that of its coat of arms—*Fluctuat Nec Mergitur...* "It rocks but does not sink..."

Projecting out into the grey waters of the Seine and dressed in all the finery of its elm and weeping willow foliage, the Pointe du Vert-Galant can be seen even better from the left bank than from the Pont des Arts. Along the bank there is a narrow quay paved with huge stones. There is no parapet to break the

harmony created between earth and sky.

This isolated point, accessible only to the pedestrian, is one of the rare oases found now and then in the city whose tentacles reach out insatiably. Only anglers and lovers meet there, or a few strollers who take time out for living.

In the background, on the Pont-Neuf—one would say on the poop if this were the prow of a ship—the proud equestrian silhouette of King Henry IV seems still to be watching over his good city of Paris.

The Pont-Neuf is the first mooring which goes from one shore to the other, cutting the point of the island. In spite of its name, it is the oldest bridge in Paris, and one of the most famous in the city's history. Begun in the reign of Henry III, it was finished by

7

Henry IV. In the course of past centuries, because it was the only bridge not lined with houses, the Pont-Neuf was the favorite meeting place for itinerant traders and mountebanks, singers and brigands. The people of Paris met there and a historian felt free to write that the Revolution was born on the Pont-Neuf.

Beyond, the Place Dauphine, which owes its name to the Dauphin who became Louis XIII, begins with two beautiful houses in exactly the same style—alternating brick and stone. Behind, the open square itself has retained some of its former peace and quiet. Book stores, art galleries, well-known "bistros" are on street level. On both sides the houses face the Seine, either the left or the right bank. Many famous Parisians of former days and of our own day have lived or live in this sheltered enclosure.

Today, the base of the triangle formed by the Place Dauphine is provided by the austere façade of the Palais de Justice whose ornate style—wide staircase,

Left: in the middle of the Pont Neuf, the statue of King Henry IV, one of the most popular figures in French history. Bottom: the tip of the Ile de la Cité. Above: a familiar view of the quays along the Seine. Below: the buildings of the Conciergerie. Following pages: various views of the Pont Neuf.

antique columns, royal lions, imperial eagles—reveals its Second Empire origin.

This Palais de Justice is multi-purpose. It forms an enormous quadrilateral that occupies this entire part of the island to the Boulevard du Palais and continues beyond in the same monumental style with the Chamber of Commerce and the Police headquarters.

Court of Summary Jurisdiction, Court of Appeal, Supreme Court of Appeal—Paris has grouped all its judiciary machinery at the former site of the palace of the Merovingian and Capetian kings, and, no doubt it was here too that the Roman governors lived. When royalty moved to the Louvre, these Courts of law took up residence. Cheek by jowl with them at the time were shops of all kinds, the last of which did not disappear until 1840. In the 17th and 18th centuries, the buildings were destroyed by fire. Most of those we see there today date from the 19th century. There is nothing really remarkable for the tourist in the imposing mass of the Palais de Justice unless it be the beautiful 18th century gilded wrought-iron gate at the entrance to the main courtyard. But the Palais de Justice houses a jewel, the Sainte-Chapelle, and it offers, at the river's edge, the picturesque

Seen from the Seine, the Pont Neuf and the Ile de la Cité. Right: views of the Pont des Arts.

ensemble of the Conciergerie whose massive outline and round towers form one of the most characteristic pictures of old Paris.

The Conciergerie's buildings which face the Seine date from the time of Philip the Fair. Until the beginning of the 17th century the waters of the river lapped the towers, which explains why alterations were made, fortunately in the original style.

In the interior, the guard-room, the men-at-arms' room and the Prisoners' gallery are interesting examples of the military architecture of the 14th century.

The Conciergerie owes its name to the "Count of the candles" who in former times was responsible for the upkeep of the buildings. Besides its architec-

tural value, it is above all the memory of those who were imprisoned there that draws visitors to the Conciergerie. Most of the victims of the Revolution were brought to this old prison, first the nobles and then the revolutionaries themselves: Danton, Desmoulins, Saint-Just, Robespierre who followed Elizabeth, the king's sister, Madame Roland de la Platière, the Countess du Barry, Philippe-Egalité who had voted for the execution of his cousin Louis XVI. Queen "Marie-Antoinette of Austria, called 'of Lorraine', widow of Louis Capet"—the entry in the prison register —spent two and a half months in her cell before being taken to the guillotine. In 1816, this cell was transformed into a chapel of atonement.

Robespierre's cell is close to the Salle des Girondins

Street scenes in the Latin Quarter. Far right: the amphitheater of Lutetia; the courtyard of the Hôtel de Cluny.

where some mementos of the victims have been gathered together. During the Revolution, there were so many prisoners in the Conciergerie that they moved about freely inside the buildings. In spite of their mental anguish, they gathered together to chat, to play and sometimes even to dance. Plots were hatched on false hopes. And every day the "tumbril" carried its cargo of condemned to the guillotine.

At the angle of the Quai de l'Horloge is the Clock Tower, also dating from the time of Philip the Fair; part of it has been reconstructed. The gilded frame was made by the sculptor Germain Pilon.

It is very unfortunate that the Sainte-Chapelle is now wedged in between the buildings of the Palais de Justice. Only one side is fully exposed, and the marve-

lous upward surge of the chapel's buttresses and spire cannot be appreciated because it is impossible to look at it in proper perspective.

Saint Louis had it built towards the middle of the 13th century, to serve as a casket for Christ's crown of thorns and fragments of the true Cross sent to him from Constantinople by two French knights, Jean de Brienne and Baudouin, during their crusade in the East.

A masterpiece of French art—not Gothic as is sometimes claimed—the Sainte-Chapelle astounds by the audacity of its conception. It dazzles by the beauty of its stained glass windows illustrating 1,134 scenes from the Old and the New Testaments and the story of the transfer of the relics. More than two thirds of

these stained glass windows are the original 13th century windows. The others were reconstituted during the monument's restoration in the 19th century. In the interior it is divided by two superimposed chapels.

Today, the relics of the Crucifixion which escaped destruction are in Notre-Dame. As a result of their removal, and perhaps also because the Sainte-Chapelle stands in the midst of administrative buildings, it seems to have lost its spiritual vocation. It is a wonderful setting for the concerts of chamber music sometimes given there—but it is no longer a sanctuary.

The whole of the city's spiritual life centers on Notre-Dame. Soul of the city, living prayer, the cathedral of Notre-Dame de Paris is the most prestigious witness of the capital's history, the most vivid evidence of French genius. Other monuments throughout the world are equally beautiful and may even be more beautiful. But there is none which combines so much nobility with so much fervor, or which expresses more eloquently the elevation of a thought (that of the architects who concieved the cathedral) and the perfection brought to its execution by the craftsmen and workers of the Middle Ages.

One is forced to conclude that this was a propitious spot for worship, for a temple was built there already in the first century. Three centuries later, the Christian faith supplanted the pagan gods, and in the 6th century Gregory of Tours was mentioning Notre-Dame. The Normans sacked the cathedral and the nearby church of Saint-Etienne. In 1160 Bishop Maurice de Sully decided that a new cathedral worthy of Paris and of his times should be built. The work, planned by an unknown architect, began in 1163 and the main part was finished in 1250.

Alterations and additions were constantly being made over the centuries, sometimes felicitous, sometimes regrettable—for instance, when contemporary taste led to the destruction of the rood-screen and the stalls, or to uncalled—for changes.

The Revolution made of the cathedral a temple to the goddess of Reason. Given back for worship in 1802, Notre-Dame was in a lamentable state. This is the building of the beginning of the 19th century, described by Victor Hugo in his famous novel *Notre-Dame of Paris*. The book's success drew attention to this example of Gothic art. A law of 1841 authorized the restoration of the Cathedral and the work, begun by Lassus was continued by Viollet-le-Duc.

In spite of its many vicissitudes, Notre-Dame of Paris today commands admiration for its perfect harmony, the unity of its original conception—something that must be apprehended before one studies

This page: the vault and stained glass windows of the oldest church in Paris, St-Séverin. The Quai des Orfèvres and the famous second-hand booksellers of the Quai Conti.

the details and the splendors of the 13th century stained glass windows, the bas-reliefs and the sculptures. Some of these sculptures are the originals, such as the one depicting the signs of the Zodiac, which show the months of the year; others have been reconstituted, for instance the images of the saints and the king's gallery, destroyed in 1793.

But the successive contributions over a period of 800 years tend to become unified in the majesty of the whole. The breadth of the interior nave—with the choir and the 12th century Gothic naves—is as remarkable as the exterior balance of its two massive towers and the delicacy of its flying buttresses, which give so much elegance to the apse.

The recent renovation of the parvis has opened up a better view of the façade. Behind, on the north side, little streets intersect at the foot of the monument. They maintain the character of intimacy in the heart of the city that the cathedral had in former days.

On the south side and behind Notre-Dame, terraces and little gardens open onto the river. A small bridge, the Pont Saint-Louis, leads to the island of the same name. In crossing the bridge, we enter a past age.

Until the early 17th century the Ile Saint-Louis—at that time consisting of two separate islets and still

Left: the buildings of the Institut de France, facing the Pont des Arts; they house, in particular, the venerable Académie Française. Bottom: the Palais du Luxembourg, home of the French Senate, and the pool of the large public gardens adjoining the palace itself.

Facing: between the Latin Quarter and the district of Saint-Germain-des-Prés, a picturesque view of the Cour de Rohan. Below: the Place de Furstenberg, one of the prettiest spots in Saint-Germain-des-Prés.

The Café de Flore, in Saint-Germain-des-Prés, and the former Café Procope, which has been famous for several centuries. Right: the belltower of the church of Saint-Germain-des-Prés.

unnamed—was a deserted place where laundry was hung up to dry and duellists sometimes clashed swords.

It was not until 1630 that the island was parcelled out on the basis of a plan put forward by Christophe Marie, an architect whose name was given to a nearby bridge. The streets were laid out without bends or turns. The rue Saint-Louis-en-l'Ile, which contains a Jesuit-style church, traverses the island from end to end. Approach streets run at right angles to the quays, named after princely families: Anjou, Bourbon, Orléans. On both sides of the river banks flanking the island, splendid residences were constructed on the paved quays.

These elegant 17th and 18th century mansions lend to the Ile Saint-Louis an aristocratic character, jealously guarded today. The hectic life of the city seems far away, and it is still possible to linger before the old mansions with their wrought-iron balconies.

After the nobles, well-to-do artists lived there: Daumier and Daubigny on the Quai d'Anjou, Philip de Champaigne, Meissonnier and Emile Bernard in the lovely house called Le Charron. Baudelaire and Theophile Gautier lived in the Lauzun, a mansion decorated by Le Brun. And Voltaire was the guest of his mistress, the Marquise du Châtelet, in the Lambert mansion.

Behind the austerely majestic façades lie peaceful courtyards. Memories float like gossamer bet-

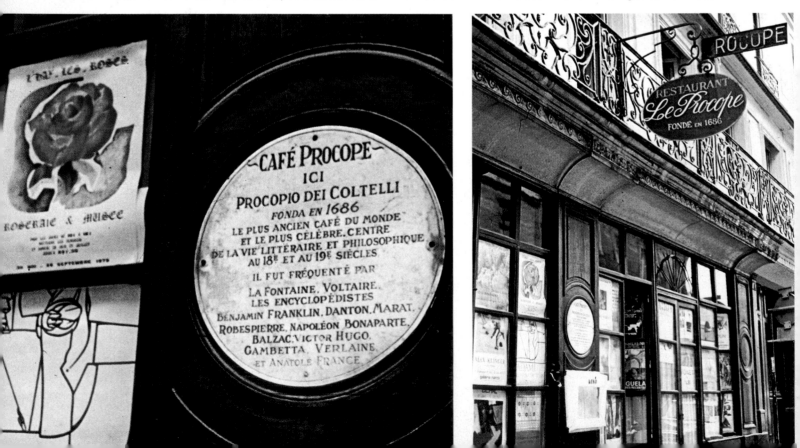

ween the old walls, and time seems to stand still when the listless noonday heat or approaching night envelops the deserted streets.

The "left bank"—a hallowed term for the Parisians—was the scene of the first extension of Paris. Its general contours lent itself to this choice. The slight elevation of the land made farming possible while the right bank was still only marshland. From the 1st century A.D. the Romans began to settle on the left bank. Despite the very few traces of their presence still remaining—the baths of Cluny and the amphitheater of Lutetia—it is the oldest quarter of Paris, since nothing is left of the first settlement on the Ile-de-la-Cité.

The roads of "New Lutetia" were rectilinear. There were some beautiful villas on the plateau behind Mont Sainte-Geneviève. But massive invasions made people abandon the Roman town, and for seven centuries the left bank was no more than a field of ruins.

At the beginning of the 12th century it came back to life, thanks to Pierre Abélard, an eminent dialectician, who left the Notre-Dame monastery, where he taught, in order to establish a community of professors and students on the slopes of Sainte-Geneviève. This community was given the name of University and the first colleges were built to lodge and teach the students.

By giving statutes to the University, Philip Augustus conferred on the left bank a character which was to be confirmed over the centuries: that of the center of Parisian intellectual life.

The colleges were religious foundations—sometimes also princely—intended more to house students than to serve as a teaching center. Jacques Hillairet writes in his *Historical Dictionary of the Streets of Paris*, "For their lessons the students left early in the morning immediately after Mass to go to Place Maubert and Rue du Fouarre where they attended open air classes, either seated on the ground or on straw. They returned to the fold only after nightfall."

At the end of the 12th century the University had three Faculties: theology, canon law, arts. Medicine was added in 1331.

The centuries have come and gone. The buildings have been replaced. Great schools have been founded which today make the area from Saint-Germain-des-Prés to the Halle-aux-Vins the veritable center of Parisian student life.

After pursuing their studies there, young people often wanted to remain faithful to the area. Thus a kind of city within the city developed. What could be called the intellectual trade started business there: book stores, publishing houses, art galleries. Many hotels opened to house foreign students. The already numerous cafés became so many literary coteries where ideas were discussed, plots were hatched and tempers became overheated. May 1968 and its barricades proved that the Latin Quarter was remaining faithful to its tradition!

Place Saint-Michel marks the entrance to the Latin

21

Above: this house (Nº 3, rue Volta) has long been considered the oldest house in Paris. Below façade of the Hôtel Fieubet, on the Quai des Célestins. Right: the ceremonial courtyard of the Hôtel Carnavalet (16th century), ornamental detail on a doorway on the Quai des Célestins, and the entrance of the Hôtel d'Almeira.

Left: niche with madonna, Hôtel de Montmorency (1743). Bottom: the Hôtel de Sens, in the Marais district which was the heart of Paris in the 17th century. Above: the splendid Place des Vosges.

Quarter. The beautiful view of Notre-Dame which it offers is one that remains in the memory. On the gray stone quays are lined the open-air bookstalls where second-hand books are sold. But, more and more, print and poster are taking the place of old editions found there in the past.

The Place Saint-Michel is one of the capital's main squares. At the far end, with its back to the corner buildings the fountain with its angel "laying the devil low" is one in name only.

From there the Boulevard Saint-Michel, known to the students as "Boul'Mich", goes straight up to the Luxembourg Garden. It was laid out from 1855 to 1859 through the section of colleges and monasteries which had been built there since the Middle Ages. From this past almost no trace remains. The celebrated cafés which had their moment of glory in the 19th century—"Vachette" at number 27, "D'Harcourt" at number 47—have themselves disappeared, victims of the changes made in modern times. Only the ruins of the baths of Cluny survive to remind us of the Roman city. A theater stood on the site of the present Lycée Saint-Louis, which itself replaced the old d'Harcourt College, demolished in 1795.

The Boulevard Saint-Michel with its nondescript buildings may not attract the lover of old stones, but it is nevertheless the liveliest, the most exciting and the most amusing of Parisian boulevards. The human fauna striding along it from dawn to dusk and all night long, is infinitely varied and light-hearted. These are the students from all countries and all races who have come to spend several years or several days breathing "the air of Paris". Since the hippy wave broke from west to north, the scene is even more picturesque. Groups form around some local figure or some solitary musician. The stalls of the many bookstores are always full of browsers.

On both sides small streets have kept their old names: Rue de la Huchette or Rue Monsieur-le-Prince. Like so many tributaries they discharge their wave of passers-by.

Boul'Mich ends at the corner of the Luxembourg Garden. Its name remains unchanged but its appearance alters, and the young people desert it. They stop at the garden whose wrought-iron gates open onto flowered lawns where beautiful ladies clad in stone dream beneath the trees. Great men also have their statues there: Chopin, Delacroix, the poet Verlaine who was an habitué of the nearby cafés, and Watteau who loved to walk in the garden while

25

thinking about the isle of Cythera.

Venerable trees give shade to the Medici fountain. Children play around the pond in which is reflected the lovely palace, built in 1615 by Queen Marie de Medici. Today it houses the Senate, after having been a prison for a very short time during the Revolution.

These attractive flower-beds have replaced very old shrubberies that had a sinister reputation in the Middle Ages. Devils haunted these spots and it took nothing less than the Carthusian monks to drive them out of the Vauvert—the green valley. All that remains of that is the familiar expression: go to the Vauvert devil!

On both sides of the Boulevard Saint-Michel, especially at the lower end, the area of the schools and colleges well deserves its name. Most of the main university buildings are located there—a tradition dating back to the Middle Ages.

The huge Louis-le-Grand lycée covers the site formerly occupied by five colleges. But it is the Sorbonne in particular that remains the pivot of Parisian university life, due to its reputation and its

On this page we see the most famous building in modern Paris: the Centre Pompidou (Beaubourg), and, right, the new Forum built on the site of the former Halles market.

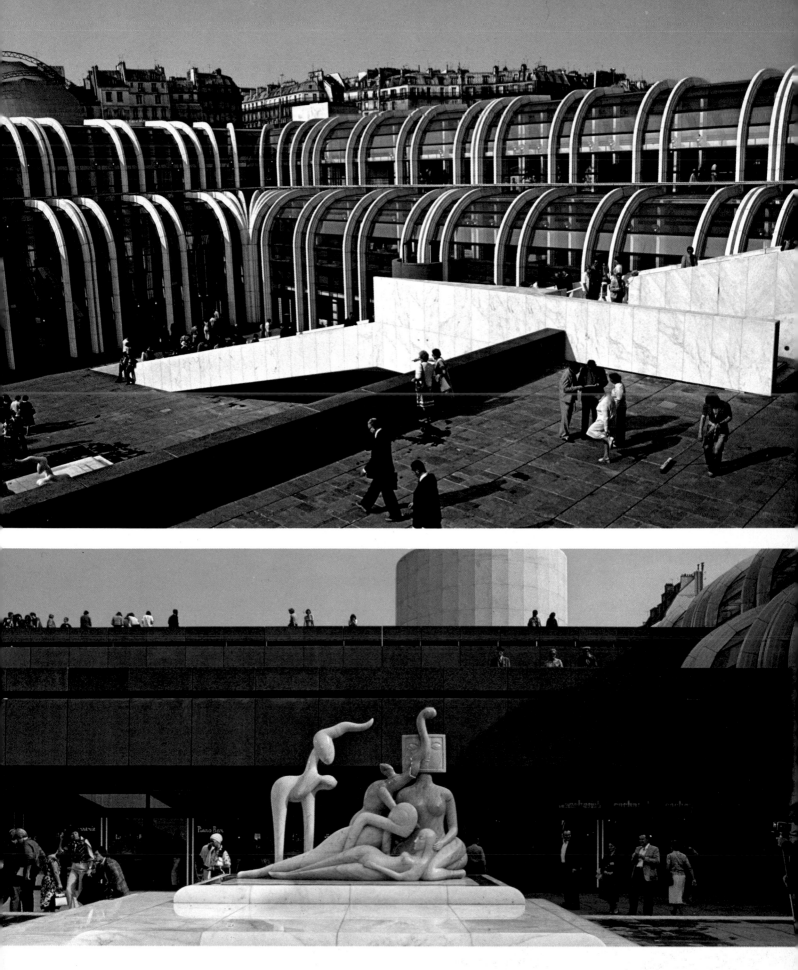

Left: the Tour St-Jacques and the Passage Vivienne. Above: the Hôtel de Soubise, in the Marais district, home of the national archives.

activity.

Its name comes from that of the founder Robert de Sorbon, Master of Theology, confessor of Saint Louis, who commissioned the first buildings, as a Faculty of Theology. Expansion was rapid and the Sorbonne became the center of the capital's intellectual life, taking part in all the religious conflicts, especially in that of the Reformation. The first French printing press was installed in the Sorbonne.

Richelieu had the buildings reconstructed. Today only the chapel remains. After the closure of the Faculty of Theology during the Revolution, the Sorbonne was used for housing. A colony of painters lived there for 15 years but the dilapidation was such that towards the end of the 19th century, new buildings had to be put up and extensions made, so that it could receive students once again. Vast lecture rooms, a library, and study rooms were built, and decorated by contemporary artists, among them Puvis de Chavanne.

The vast square which occupies the 'summit' (all of 195 feet!) of what is still called Mont Sainte-Geneviève is dominated by the imposing mass of the Pantheon. The Pantheon was originally a church, erected by Louis XV on the plans of the architect Soufflot, to replace the early Gothic church of Sainte-Geneviève. Finished at the beginning of the Revolution, the new edifice was not used for worship because it was decreed by the Constituent Assembly that it should become a place of burial for great

Frenchmen. The two towers were demolished and the windows blocked up. Mirabeau was buried in the Pantheon, and at a later date the remains of Voltaire and Rousseau were transferred there.

Napoleon gave the Pantheon back for worship. Louis-Philippe annulled the decree that had turned it into a monument to the dead. The future Napoleon III made a basilica of it, but the Third Republic once again took it away from the Church in order to receive there in great pomp the coffin of Victor Hugo. Generals and scientists, scholars, ministers and admirals, Zola and Jaurès came to join Voltaire, Rousseau and Hugo.

Neither the columns nor the dome, nor the big blind walls are conducive to the best effect. The size of the building accentuates the heaviness of the plan. In the northeast angle of the square is the Church of Saint-Etienne du Mont, in flamboyant Gothic style, and containing a 16th century rood screen, the only one still extant in a Paris church. The poet Racine is buried there. After the expulsion of the Jansenists, his body was exhumed with those of several monks of the Port-Royal des Champs Abbey.

Parallel to the Boulevard Saint-Michel, coming from the Petit-Pont de la Cité, the Rue Saint-Jacques reaches the plateau of the Pantheon and continues beyond towards the Palais-Royal. This winding street, with its old houses, gives us some idea of 18th century Paris.

Let us go back in time. In the Middle Ages this was

One of the colonnades of the Place du Palais-Royal. Below: the remarkable architectural ensemble formed by the church of Saint-Germain l'Auxerrois and a former mansion which has now become the town hall of the 1st arrondissement of Paris. Right: one of the vaults of Saint-Germain l'Auxerrois.

Left-hand page: various views of the Palais du Louvre and the Arc du Carrousel. Bottom: the noble harmony of the buildings on the Place Vendôme. Above: the Paris opera house.

the path which the pilgrims took on their way to Compostela in Spain, the birthplace of Saint James of Compostela; hence the great number of monasteries and convents that were established in the vicinity. Of these practically nothing now remains. Further back in time it was a Roman road, one of the great carrefours of the thousand year old capital city.

Curiously, its surroundings, even in their most modern aspect, seem to maintain a tradition. Down the centuries young people have cherished their prerogatives and their ways, and it is easy to believe that there is not such a great distance between the "escholier" (scholar) of former times whose stamping ground was the Rue du Fouarre and the hippies of today who established their "HQ" on the little island of Saint-Severin.

Between the quay and the Boulevard Saint-Germain the old streets with their evocative names—de la Huchette, de la Harpe, de la Parcheminerie—form one of the most picturesque and cosmopolitan corners of Paris. The restaurants are Italian, Arab, Greek, Chinese, Japanese. Small studio cinemas are found in profusion. Fashionable little restaurants where old French songs can be heard are to be found in medieval cellars.

The Church of Saint-Severin was the University church. With its sculptured portal, the double ambulatory, and the stained glass windows it offers an admirable example of 13th to 15th century Gothic art. Concerts are given there and also in the nearby cloister and the adjoining garden which covers over a former burial place.

Closer to the quay is the church of Saint-Julian-le-Pauvre, parts of which have survived from the original 12th century building. The little square surrounding the church offers an unforgettable view of Notre-Dame of Paris. In the square is the oldest tree in Paris, dating from the reign of Louis XIV.

Above: the quays along the Seine opposite the gardens of the Palais Royal. Below: the gardens of the Palais Royal, with a view of the obelisk on the Place de la Concorde, and, beyond the Champs-Elysées, the Arc de Triomphe on the Etoile. Right: the Place de la Concorde — the heart of Paris.

Past the Boulevard Saint-Germain, the Rue Saint-Jacques becomes more austere between the high walls of the Sorbonne and the lycées. Beyond the Pantheon one can still find a good many 18th century houses and mansions, their façades often in a very bad state of repair.

Almost nothing of the convents remains except the portal of the Carmelite convent, to which Louise de La Vallière retired after being abandoned by King Louis XIV.

In the hope of being able to withdraw now and then from the intrigues of the Court and forget her royal husband Louis XIII's infidelities, Anne of Austria built the Church of Val-de-Grâce whose vast Italian-style chapel opens onto the Rue Saint-Jacques. Val-de-Grâce became a military hospital but the church has survived the centuries without damage. For a long time the hearts of the queen and others members of the royal family were kept there. At the time of the Revolution the lead caskets containing them were melted down and the hearts, so it is claimed, were acquired by the painter Drolling. It seems that the organic matter, mixed with oil, gave a brown color of incomparable brilliance. Whether or not this claim is justified can be judged from several of this artist's paintings, hanging in the Church of Saint-Sulpice.

The Place du Pantheon is a good point of departure for wandering around in the little streets that go down towards the Jardin des Plantes. The most interesting of these is the Rue Mouffetard, as much for its many old houses and amusing signboards as for the bustling activity in its food stores. The time to see it is in the morning at market time. The traders' stalls overflow onto the sidewalks. The smells of the "fruit and vegetable" stalls mingle with that of "fresh fish" whose savor and price are loudly praised by the traders to all within earshot. Without doubt these are the last of those "cries of Paris" which, in the 19th century, filled the streets of the capital.

Sometimes an itinerant band can be heard. Between the Place de la Contrescarpe and the Church of Saint-Médard there is a constant coming and going of the real 'common people' of Paris.

As at Saint-Severin, the number of restaurants, above all, of oriental restaurants, is legion. Mouffetard also has its theater and its cabarets, frequented by a sometimes surprising public. Into the Rue Mouffetard pour the crowds from the nearby streets, whose delectable names tell of the days of the not-too-distant past: Rue du Pot-de-Fer (iron pot), Rue de l'Epée-de-Bois (wooden sword), Rue de l'Arbalète (crossbow) and, farther on, the Rue du Puits-de-l'Ermite (hermit's well). Anyone wanting to get to the heart of working-class Paris owes himself a stroll through the neighborhood.

The Place de la Concorde and the Champs-Elysées illuminated by night.

Left: the wrought-iron gate of the "Coq" and the Palais de l'Elysée. This gate is opened only once every seven years, on the occasion of the election of the President of the Republic. Bottom: the inner courtyard of the Palais de l'Elysée. Above: view of the Avenue des Champs-Elysées.

At the bottom of the Rue Mouffetard, the Church of Saint-Médard is hidden beneath the trees in a small square. It also has a long history, dating back to the 12th century, but it was rebuilt in the 15th and again in the 18th century. The blend of Gothic and Renaissance styles is not a happy one. The square occupies the site of the former cemetery, scene in the 18th century of the weird revels of the Convulsionaries of Saint-Médard.

In the 1860s, a wide street was constructed through this quarter, the Rue Monge, which joins the Boulevard Saint-Germain at the Avenue des Gobelins. The making of this road led to the discovery of the amphitheater of Lutetia, which for ten centuries had been lost even to memory. It was restored and a square was laid out around it. When the inhabitants of New Lutetia withdrew to the Ile-de-la-Cité, the Roman stones were taken away for the construction of a wall. Later on others were used to build houses, and consequently, the amphitheater as reconstituted can now give only a vague idea of the size of the original structure, which was both amphitheater and theater. Today open air performances are sometimes organized there.

Well worth a visit in this quarter are the Mosque and its Turkish baths, the Halle-aux-Vins (wine market),

part of which has already been transferred to make way for the Faculty of Sciences, now largely installed on the site, and finally the Jardin des Plantes which abuts on the Seine. Thanks to Henry IV and the Duke of Sully, it is both botanical garden and zoological park. The renowned naturalist Buffon developed it in the 17th century and made it an incomparable center for the study of flora and fauna from all over the world.

The area between the Seine and the Luxembourg Garden, on the side of the Boulevard Saint-Michel opposite the school area, is the unchallenged domain of writers and those who live from the activity of writers—the editors and the bookstores. In short, the young university student has only to cross the boulevard in order to find himself, as a grown-up, at the Place de l'Odéon. Several steps farther on—if fate should smile on him—he could, as an old man, be seated under the famous symbol of the French Academy, the cupola of the Palais de l'Institut.

The entire, literary life of Paris flourishes in this confined space. Through this melting pot, where for so many centuries so many illustrious, unforgettable figures have lived and died, there passes, almost of necessity, everything that French thought gives to the world. The poles of attraction change

39

Three of the avenues which radiate from the Place de l'Etoile (now Place Charles-de-Gaulle): on the left is the famous Avenue Foch, which leads to the Bois de Boulogne, and is regarded as the most aristocratic thoroughfare in the capital. Right: the Arc de Triomphe, and, bottom, the Tomb of the Unknown Soldier with a view of the Champs-Elysées.

with time. At the end of the 19th century the sector around the Odéon was, *par excellence*, that of writers and poets. Verlaine and Mallarmé could be seen there. After the second World War, Saint-Germain-des-Prés assumed the mantle of the Odéon's glory. Philosophers, singers and song-writers settled there. The cellar replaced the café but the celebrities met each other just as much in the cellars, towing disciples and devotees in their wake.

The sixth arrondissement or ward of Paris, the one we are interested in here, has its zones of action. Between the Seine and the Boulevard Saint-Germain, beyond the islet which still has a welcome for the "student race", lies the artists' quarter, as can be deduced from the name of one of its streets, the Rue Saint-André-des-Arts. Here too one finds those who dream of becoming artists, the turbulent "quat' zarts" (four arts). The celebrated balls which they gave have gone down in history. Their school, a part of which is the former Petits-Augustins monastery, is on the Rue Bonaparte. The main courtyard is oddly formed, from a façade of the Château d'Anet, a portico of the Château de Gaillon and the remains of demo-

lished mansions.

On the other side of the Boulevard Saint-Germain, under the protection of the two towers of Saint-Sulpice religion holds sway. Here religious books, sacred ornaments, statues, etc. are sold.

Around the Church of Saint-Germain-des-Prés, one of the oldest and historically most moving churches in Paris, are the literary cafés, each with its share of customers. Cellars, no longer so fashionable, are hidden away in the nearby streets. The local fauna, no longer calling itself existentialist (though it probably is), is reading Sartre and Boris Vian. But amid the tumult of this around-the-clock life, there are two havens of peace and provincial charm, the Cour de

The bridges of Paris add to the city's beauty. On this page we see some of the more famous ones: the Pont du Carrousel, the Pont de la Concorde and, below, the Pont Alexandre III. Right: view of Les Invalides and the esplanade from the Pont Alexandre III; the Eiffel Tower, seen from the Palais de Chaillot. Following pages: general view of central Paris.

One of the most modern districts in Paris is the Front de Seine; above, one of its tower blocks. Below and right: the Palais de Chaillot and the Trocadero.

Three of the most famous restaurants in Paris, both past and present: Maxim's, Lapérouse *and* Drouant *(noted also as the scene of the annual award of the Prix Goncourt).*
Following pages: some of the many fine gastronomic establishments in the capital.

Rohan whose gates are closed at night and the Place Furstenberg, where Delacroix had his studio in a garden hemmed in by high, centuries-old buildings.

The Church of Saint-Germain-des-Prés is all that remains of the famous abbey of Saint-Germain, which was at the origin of the area's development. The church is one of the rare examples in Paris of 11th and 12th century architecture. Its square tower surmounted by twin arcades has the charm of a village church. The nave, which was painted in the 19th century, is in a beautiful style. The chancel is one of the first examples of Gothic art. Mabillon, Boileau and Descartes are three of the great men who have been buried here.

On the right bank of the river, the face of Paris changes. Let us look for this new face in the heart of the city first of all, in the capital's overpopulated, busiest and most commercial areas.

There are two main ways of reaching the Opéra from the Bastille. To reach the Place de l'Opéra the first of these, parallel to the Seine, forks right at the Palais-Royal. The second makes a semi-circular curve at the Monument de la République and the Grands Boulevards, following approximately the outline of Charles V's old city wall, as enlarged by Louis XIII.

The Paris of the first route is still the Paris of history, not of the first thousand years but of the second. No longer the Paris of convents and schools but instead of monarchy and revolutions. Down the centuries the Bastille, the Hôtel-de-Ville, the Tuileries, the Palais-Royal have all seen coaches pass and barricades go up.

The area around the second route is the Paris of business. Here is to be found every kind of trade and enterprise: the tailors of Sentier and the printers of Croissant, the shopkeepers of the Temple (the church of the Knights Templars), the bankers and stockbrokers and the artisans of the Faubourg Saint-Antoine. This is the domain of the people of Paris who, depending on the hour, pursue their work or their pleasures along the Grands Boulevards.

Although Baron Haussmann undertook major demolition work in order to lay out rectilinear avenues in the maze of small streets, traffic is still a problem, while the crowds grow ever denser.

These big boulevards had their day of glory. They retain a certain air of Second Empire and Belle Epoque, at least on the façades of their buildings. At that time this was the center of Parisian entertainment. From the Opéra to the variety shows, from the Folies-Bergère to the Café Napolitain one came across the carriages and horses of that society which Marcel Proust watched die. The cafés, restaurants and theaters remain but they have followed the fashion of the day and often lost their glamour.

Between the Grands Boulevards and the Châtelet, two other districts have their place in Parisian history, the Marais, still rich in beautiful dwellings and the Halles (food markets) which Zola called the "stomach of Paris". The recent move of the Halles to Rungis in southern Paris has been filled by a superbly imaginative shopping and cultural complex called the Forum.

Another page has been turned and so, day after day, images of Paris vanish.

A turntable in the east of Paris, the Place de la Bastille is the capital's working class crossroads just as the Place de l'Etoile, to the west, is the aristocratic one.

A number of roads converge towards the Place de la Bastille. It is crossed by the Rue Saint-Antoine and the Rue du Faubourg Saint-Antoine which was the way always taken by the revolutionary crowds pouring towards the royal residences of the Louvre or the Tuileries.

For the Parisian people, the name Bastille symbolizes the victory of freedom, a victory that is commemorated, as the French national holiday, on July 14th, the date in 1789 when the crowds stormed and took the Bastille, then a State prison. The taking of the Bastille was itself, in fact, no more than symbolic, for only seven uninteresting brigands were found in the cells. But the prison had held illustrious inmates, and in the people's eyes it symbolized

RESTAURANT CHINOIS

"AU BON COIN"

ISON CATHERINE

LA MÈRE CATHERINE RESTAURANT

COMMUNE LIBRE du vieux MONTMARTRE

LA MÈRE CATHERINE

TABAC

PATISSERIE TUNISIENNE

PATISSERIE

SANDWICHES

Pigalle and the Place Blanche... At the threshold of Montmartre and the district of pleasure and excitement, the famous Moulin Rouge, seen by night and day, and also through the eyes of one of the numerous painters who frequented this area.

royal despotism. The Bastille was demolished stone by stone and nothing remains of this fortress except some markings on the paving stones.

The column which rises there, called Column of the Bastille or Column of July, was erected in memory of those stormy July days in 1830, when King Charles was dethroned. According to one historian the Faubourg Saint-Antoine was "the crater from which revolutionary lava most often escapes."

In the northern part especially, the visitor who loves old stones, will find much to move him. Every street and almost every house in this area has its history, recalling the memory of some great lord or some noble lady of former times.

It was to Henry IV, "first town-planner of Paris", that the Marais owed its development. The creation of the Place Royale and the parcelling out of the surrounding lands were at the origin of the aristocratic expansion of the area. This expansion continued in the 17th century, under the reign of Louis XIII, which explains the imposing appearance of so many private homes that are more like palaces.

To the south of Rue Saint-Antoine, near the Seine, the Sens residence is one of the oldest. It was built at the end of the 15th century for the Archbishop of Sens—who at that time was responsible for the diocese of Paris. The residence was later offered by Henry IV to his first wife, the celebrated Queen Margot. It then fell into ruins, until its restoration in 1935-1936 by the city of Paris. It now offers an interesting example of the French secular architecture of its period.

A picture for one's souvenir photo album: the top of the Butte Montmartre with the domes of the basilica of Sacré-Cœur.
Bottom: the town hall of the 'free commune' of Montmartre. Actually the commune has no legal existence, but the authorities have always protected it, particularly on account of the festivities for which it is noted.
Below: one of the last authentic mills on the Butte.
Right: a famous street on the Butte: rue St-Rustique.

Very close by, the small Rue de Birague opens onto the Place des Vosges—formerly called the Place Royale—one of the most attractive squares in Paris, because of the beautiful layout of its Louis XIII mansions of brick and stone, with their large slate roofs, doors opening to the north and the south and the arcades around the square, where children play.

From the Bastille, a séries of boulevards lead to the Opera. When they reach another focal point of Parisian life, the Place de la République, these streets take the more familiar name of Grands Boulevards. Landmarks on this route to the Opéra are the two portals, which are in fact two triumphal arches, Porte Saint-Denis and Porte Saint-Martin erected in 1672 and 1674 respectively, to commemorate the victories of Louis XIV.

The most famous Parisian theaters were and still are located along the stretch from the Boulevard du Temple to the Boulevard des Capucines. The Boulevard du Temple was given the name "crime boulevard" because of the bloody melodramas performed there last century for the people's entertainment.

Farther west the repertory became more attractive, and it was on the stages of the 'Nouveautés' and the 'Gymnase' that boulevard comedy was born in which de Flers, Caillavet, Bernstein and Guitry shone.

The Grands Boulevards still draw the Parisian crowds and foreigners, much more for their attractions and entertainments than for the Second Empire architecture of their buildings or their historic memories.

From the Rue Saint-Antoine via the Rue de Rivoli, the great east-west thoroughfare reaches the Hôtel de Ville, whose square borders the Seine to the south and gives access, by the Arole bridge, to the Ile-de-la-Cité.

The Place de l'Hôtel de Ville was formerly the Place de Grève, which sloped gently down towards the river and was the center of a busy traffic of merchandise brought by boat from Burgundy. From the Middle Ages to the end of the 18th century, the Square was the scene of executions by hanging, quartering and beheading! A number of notorious criminals perished there—Ravaillac, the Marquise de Brinvilliers (the poisoner), Cartouche—and revolutionaries like Fouquier-Tinville. The Place de Grève was also a silent witness to events at the Hôtel de Ville during the revolutions of the 19th century and beyond, culminating in the liberation of Paris in 1944.

The impressive Hôtel de Ville, which occupies one whole side of the Square, was reconstructed in 1882, in Renaissance style, covered with little ornamental turrets and statues. It replaced the previous building, burnt down during the 1871 Commune.

One of the old coffee houses which abound in Montmartre: the premises of the former 'Lapin à Gill' cabaret, famous during the Butte's heyday. An inn on the Place du Tertre and the permanent exhibition of paintings to be seen on the square.

Very close by, next to the Place du Châtelet, is the Saint-Jacques Tower, all that remains of the famous church Saint-Jacques la Boucherie (Saint James the Butcher's). It is a handsome Gothic tower, the only vestige of former days in this area where once there stood another fortified castle, the Grand Châtelet; they date from the 19th century, i.e. they are without style or grandeur. To find these qualities again, one must follow the Rue de Rivoli to the Louvre. Although the various buildings of this vast ensemble were erected over a long period, from the 15th to the 19th centuries, they present a certain unity. Around the square courtyard and the Square du Carrousel are Perrault's Colonnade and the covered walk at the edge of the water as well as the Pavillons de Flore and de l'Horloge which house the Finance Ministry, the Decorative Arts Museum and above all the Louvre, one of the most prestigious museums in the world.

The description of the palace and museum buildings would in itself fill one whole volume! By turns a fortified castle, a princely residence, a royal palace, academies, workshops, a museum, in former times the Louvre was closed in by the Tuileries palace. Only the Pavillon de Marsan was reconstructed to correspond to the Pavillon de Flore bordering the quays.

All that remained of the Tuileries, burned down in 1871, are the lovely gardens created by Catherine de Medici and redesigned by Le Nôtre in the 17th century. Here are flower beds, ornamental lakes and many statues (mainly by Aristide Maillol) on the lawns close to the Arc-de-Triomphe du Carrousel.

Facing the Louvre, the Place du Palais-Royal gives access to the garden of the same name. At the time of Cardinal Richelieu, who commissioned both palace and garden, it opened behind the buildings which today house the Council of State. In 1781 the Duke of Orleans had the idea of enclosing the garden between the covered passage-ways used for business purposes and the buildings used for housing. This idea did not appeal to the property owners in the neighboring streets since it meant that they would be deprived of a view of the garden.

Later on the wooden arcades, put up 'temporarily', became a refuge for gamblers, rakes and pickpockets. When this 'fashionable society' was forced to leave because of the construction of the last arcades in 1829, the vitality of the Palais-Royal began to decline. For a short time the reputation of the Second Empire picked it up but in 1907 it had become so deserted that it was no more than a meeting place for hooligans. Today it is one of the most delightful havens in Paris.

Just to pass through the beautiful main courtyard is to discover the peace and quiet of days gone by, only a stone's throw from traffic lights, traffic jams and turmoil. Calm follows tumult, silence follows uproar. Children play, pigeons fly, an old man dreams and lovers embrace in front of the flowered lawns.

A 'rampart' of buildings is enough to create a privileged haven of peace and quiet. A beautiful example from the past, but one which today's architects have not yet been inspired to copy and so make the new cities habitable.

Round about, under the arcades, the boutiques (selling stamps and medals) do not attract crowds. One seems to see Colette and Jean Cocteau standing at the windows overlooking the shops, for they were the last famous inhabitants of the Palais-Royal.

Montparnasse and its famous coffee houses which, even more than those of Montmartre, still contain the memories of so many great painters of the Impressionist period: La Rotonde, Le Dôme *and* La Coupole. *Right: the Tour Montparnasse, the tallest building in Europe. Following pages: general view, showing the Ecole Militaire, the Eiffel Tower, the Palais de Chaillot, the Arc de Triomphe and Les Invalides.*

At the corner of this square, the Comédie-Française, is the official stage on which the glories of repertory are enacted. For the past 300 years the greatest French actors have performed at the Comédie.

When it leaves the Place du Théâtre-Français, the Avenue de l'Opéra goes off diagonally from the temple of Thalia and Melpomene to that of Euterpe and Terpsichore. The Opéra is older than the avenue leading to it, having been constructed by Garnier during the Second Empire, at a time when architecture was looking in antique property shops for a style. The most remarkable of the sculptures which decorate it is *Dance* by Carpeaux.

The very busy intersection of the Place de l'Opéra connects the Grands Boulevards with the Place de la Concorde and the business sectors to the north (travel agencies, business and insurance offices, etc.), with the area parallel to the Seine. In the subterranean Paris of the 'metro' we also find a busy intersection, this time of underground railway lines leading to all the points of the capital.

A large pond marks the end of the garden of the Tuileries towards the west. Children sail their miniature boats in it and some long-haired tourists soak their tired feet in it.

Beyond the pond, on each side, a ramp goes up to the terrace which bounds the garden from the Rue de Rivoli to the Seine embankment. There are two buildings on the terrace; one used to be the Jeu de Paume, the other the orangery of the former palace of the Tuileries. They have become art museums. The first is devoted to works of the 19th century—the "golden century" of French painting—from paintings by Corot and the landscape artists of his time to the Impressionists and Post-Impressionists, with Renoir, Monet, Cezanne, Van Gogh, Gauguin rooms and works by Toulouse-Lautrec, Degas, Seurat, etc. Too small to house all the riches of its collection, the Jeu de Paume museum is one of the high places of French art.

The Orangerie is reserved for the most prestigious temporary exhibitions, devoted to a School or an artist. These exhibitions are exceptional events. The Van Gogh exhibition in 1972 was seen by more than half a million visitors in a few months.

The only pictures hung permanently are the Nymphéas of Claude Monet, poems in color. Here the painter has recorded for all time the ephemeral flowering of his Giverny garden.

After leaving these museums, the visitor needs to reflect upon what he has seen. There are chairs under the trees on the terrace. Several meters high, the terrace dominates the vast Place de la Concorde and that famous panorama stretching to the Louvre on one side and to the Arc de l'Etoile on the other.

An unflagging procession of cars turns around the Obelisk in one continuous strident sound, toned down by the size of the site. The tourist from Pennsylvania, the 'hippy' from Stockholm, the student from Vienna lean on the white stone balustrade dreaming of

Facing: a lane in the old town of Passy, which has remained unchanged for centuries.

Right: the Roseraie de Bagatelle and the courtyard of a mansion in the 16th arrondissement.

France's past—or perhaps of their own loves.

La Place de la Concorde. It has been said that it is one of the most beautiful places in the world. This may very well be true, because of the harmonious architectural conception. The beauty comes less from the buildings bounding the Place on its north side than from the sense of vastness lent to the scene by the imaginative planning of Gabriel. Sky and space are elements of the setting as much as the severe beauty of the palaces and the fantasy of the fountains.

The Place de la Concorde was designed and built under Louis XV, the "Well-Beloved", and it was offered to him by the magistrates of Paris. At that time there was marshland beyond the garden of the Tuileries. Constructed on the plans of the architect Gabriel, the Square was finished in 1753. The building of the palaces lasted from 1760 to 1775. Fittingly, it was given the name Place Louis XV. The decorations came later. There are the horses called Marly—after the castle from which they were taken—at the beginning of the Champs-Elysées; the obelisk from Luxor, presented to Louis-Philippe in 1830 by Mehemet Ali dates from the time of Ramses II, 13 centuries before Christ; the two illuminated fountains and the austere figures at the corners which symbolize several cities of France. Victor Hugo's friend Juliet Drouet posed for Pradier's representation of Strasbourg.

On both sides of the axis perpendicular to that of the Tuileries, the view is obstructed by two buildings which are rather clumsy imitations of antique architecture: the Church of the Madeleine to the north and the Chamber of Deputies to the south. On January 21, 1793 Louis XVI was guillotined at the Place de la Concorde, then known as the Place "de la Revolution". Fifteen hundred years of French royalty came to an end with his death, certainly forever. However triumphant at the time, the two empires that represented France's return to the monarchy in the 19th century seem no more than "incidental happenings" appealing to those nostalgic for the past and the glossy magazines. Neither of these regimes managed to attain its majority.

In 1823 the Place was baptized Place Louis XVI in memory of the guillotined King, but it soon resumed the name of Concorde given to it by the Republic. No name is more likely to erase the dramas of which it was the theater.

With many other 'royal' names, the name of the Rue Royale (which continues to the Madeleine from the Place de la Concorde) reminds us that republican France neither forgets nor disowns its past. The luxury establishments of this famous street also stamp it as royal: boutiques, cafés and that famous restaurant 'Maxim's' which has been frequented for

almost a century by celebrities from all over the world.

Beyond the Rue Royale and the Madeleine extend the very busy avenues and streets of the Saint-Augustin, Saint-Lazare and Europe sectors, all the way to the 'exterior' boulevards and the delightful Parc Monceau.

Between the Tuileries and the Opera, the Place Vendôme demands a visit. Its architectural harmony makes it one of the most perfect of Squares. It was created by Jules Hardouin-Mansart as a setting worthy of Louis XIV's statue which was to occupy the center. Precision and majesty worthy of the "Sun King's" century, the buildings themselves remain as they were created. But in the course of the centuries the decorative design has undergone as many transformations as the Panthéon!

The Rue de la Paix extends from there to the Opéra. It is a 'royal' road of luxury shops—fashions, jewelry, etc.

But the Rue du Faubourg-Saint-Honoré is also very much worth a visit, to discover the aristocratic shops of France's capital city—boutiques, haute couture, art galleries, jewelers', all catching the attention by their attractive window display, and holding it by the magic of their wares. The Rue du Faubourg-Saint-Honoré is next door to the Palais de l'Elysée, the presidential residence, whose splendors are jealously guarded from the gaze of the passer-by! And the guard, a sentinel in ceremonial uniform, watches over the safety and the serenity of the head of State.

It is also called "the most famous avenue in the world". It was laid out in 1670 by Le Nôtre, the genius of the royal gardens, to create a prospect that came into its own only 150 years later. But one has the impression that the ideas of the Grand Siècle had foreknowledge of the future.

Around the avenue of elms there were at the time only garden-allotments and thickets. Open-air restaurants and taverns were opened, but at the beginning of the 19th century they were not yet very safe. The 'Coliseum', a huge complex intended for a variety of entertainments could hold 40,000 people. Then came the Winter Garden, the Castle of Flowers,

In the heart of the Plaine Monceau (which corresponds to the 17th arrondissement of Paris and is, after the 16th and Neuilly, one of the most fashionable residential areas in the capital), the Parc Monceau.

Above: the Naumachia in the Parc Monceau and, right, one of the wrought-iron gates of the garden.

One of the most famous places in working-class Paris: the locks of the St-Martin canal. Below: a typical coffee house in old Belleville. Right: view of the garden of the Buttes Chaumont, to the north of Paris.

the Summer Circus, the Alcazar, etc. The Champs-Elysées was given over wholly to the diversion of the Parisians.

The lower part, near the Place de la Concorde, kept its character of court promenade. It still has it and it is only at the roundabout that the avenue itself opens up between the ill-matched buildings where the decades rub shoulders with each other. The style of the Second Empire and that of 1925 are gradually being swallowed up by the modernism of concrete and glass. The aristocratic mansions of the "Belle Epoque" have been supplanted by offices, cinemas and *drugstores*. The Champs-Elysées is the privileged domain of the film world, which holds its meetings, shows its successes and keeps its dreams alive there. 'Fouquet's', the biggest café on the avenue remains the meeting place of producers, scenario-writers and actors. In the 50's the popular Raimu was the hero, surrounded by a court of intimates and courtesans.

Scraggy trees partly hide the irregular façades. Flags flutter in the wind at each visit of foreign heads of State. Rectilinear and wide, the avenue of the Champs-Elysées cries out for parades. Until recently that of July 14th was a tradition. The 'victory parades' in 1919 and 1945 have remained famous. The Cossacks were seen there in 1814 and the Nazis

in 1940. In the eyes of the world the Champs-Elysées epitomizes Paris.

The Etoile is at the top of the avenue. It is a majestic square, from which radiate, in perfect symmetry, 12 wide avenues with names recalling Napoleon's victories and the memory of illustrious Field Marshals. In the center is the Arc-de-Triomphe whose towering form dominated the skyline before the buildings of the Défense came to disturb the harmony.

In 1806, shortly after the Battle of Austerlitz, Napoleon ordered the Arc-de-Triomphe to be erected to the glory of his armies, but the work was not finished until 30 years later. In 1840 this triumphal arch was a silent witness of the procession bringing back the emperor's ashes from St. Helena. In 1885 Victor Hugo's huge catafalque was placed there for a night and, since 1921, the body of an unknown soldier, fallen during the First World War, has rested there under the eternal flame of remembrance.

The finest of the sculptures on the façades of the Arc-de-Triomphe, by François Rude, is "The Departure of the Volunteers", more commonly known as "La Marseillaise".

The Place de l'Etoile is the focal point of the glorious figures in France's military history. That is why Charles de Gaulle's name has been added.

Triumph is but transient; its price is misfortune and death. Napoleon's tomb is in the central crypt of the Church of the Dôme, which has a magnificent gilded cupola, in the Cour d'Honneur of the Hôtel des Invalides.

The beautiful architectural ensemble of the Invalides is situated on the left bank of the Seine, beyond the Alexander III bridge, the finest bridge in Paris. A vast esplanade leads up to it. Today, the Hôtel des Invalides houses an Army museum and two churches, in one of which, the Dôme, are also the tombs of Napoleon's two brothers, several marshals of the Empire as well as those of Vauban, Foch and de Lyautey. Napoleon's tomb of porphyry and green granite is surrounded by twelve figures representing twelve of his victories.

A stone's throw from the Place Vauban, onto which the Invalides opens, is the Military Academy, which reinforces the 'métier' of this sector of Paris. Louis XV had it built at the request of Madame de Pompadour. From the beginning it was destined for the training of future officers. Bonaparte spent a year at the Academy and later installed his imperial guard there. It is now once again fulfilling its original purpose.

For the past 20 years, behind its buildings, has stood the modern architecture of the UNESCO palace. It was planned by architects of three nationalities, an Italian, an American and a Frenchman. The decoration too was entrusted to artists from different countries:

Two famous squares, each adorned with a noble column, from the eastern part of Paris: the Place de la Bastille and the Place de la Nation. Right: one of the famous establishments of 'Paris canaille' (rue de Lappe).

Calder, Le Corbusier, Lurçat, Picasso, Miro, Bazaine, Artigas, Tamayo, Isamu, Noguchi and others. The Palace houses, among other services, the libraries, conference halls, etc.

On the other side of the Military Academy is the vast esplanade of the Champs-de-Mars, whose lawns and shaded lanes extend to the foot of the Eiffel Tower, whose metal silhouette seems to disappear into the sky. The Tower is the most popular touristic attraction in Paris and the best-known monument in the world. For a long time it was a subject of controversy for the Parisians themselves. It is on three levels or platforms, each floor being open to the public.

The first has a snack bar and a restaurant. On the third floor a special stamp cancelling service is available to philatelists. The same floor also houses radio and TV transmitters. The last aerial, installed in 1957, brought the Tower's overall height to 1040 feet.

Jean Cocteau had no hesitation in comparing the Eiffel Tower with Notre-Dame de Paris: "It is the Notre-Dame of the left bank. It is the queen of Paris." Its visitors are counted by the millions every year. From the different platforms, the eye takes in the sweep of Paris, the suburbs, the distant forests of the Ile-de-France. At the foot of the Tower on the right bank are the gardens of the Trocadero with their terraced fountains. On the terraces in front of the two wings of the Palais du Chaillot is a double row of modern statues. This palace is one of the most recently built in Paris. It was constructed in 1937 after the demolition of the former Trocadero whose Moresque-casino style was regretted by no one! A vast square separates the two wings and affords a beautiful view of the left bank. The Palais du Chaillot houses several museums: The Museum of Man, the

71

Navy Museum, the Museum of French Monuments; there is a Film-library—that 'shrine' of the devotees of the 'Seventh Art'—and the theater which was the Théâtre National Populaire where Gérard Philipe, Jean Vilar and their co-stars had great success and whose creative acting marked an epoch in the history of the theater.

Montmartre and Montparnasse are undoubtedly the two best known areas of Paris. They represent two poles of the city's intellectual life whose influence has spread over the Old and the New World, two stages of development that have become epochs in the history of art.

Counterbalancing each other, these two areas are approximately equidistant from the Seine. The first is on the right bank, the second on the left. Montmartre, more correctly called the 'Butte Montmartre' or simply the Butte (Mound) is really a 'mount', but the Mont of Montparnasse is only symbolic, the reference being to Mount Parnassus, the name given to it in the 17th century by the students

Above: this church is typical of the 'villages' of old Paris: Saint-Pierre de Charonne. Left: the tower blocks of the modern district of the Place d'Italie. Right: the front of this food store preserves the refinement of traditional French style.

of rubbish, which was removed many years ago. of the Latin Quarter. This 'mount' was only a mound

Nobody can quite explain just why the 'vie de Bohème' has emigrated from one 'mound' to the other in the course of the last 100 years. From the end of the 19th century to the first World War, Montmartre enjoyed the attentions of the Press and was the magnetic pole towards which the artists gravitated. Then cosmopolitanism took a hand and around 1910 Montparnasse began to be the meeting place for the aesthetes. The 'Lapin à Gill' was abandoned for 'La Rotonde', the 'Bateau-Lavoir', for 'Cité Falguière' until the last war led to a new exodus towards Saint-Germain-des-Prés.

These 'migratory' movements in the so-called artistic life of Paris were accompanied by a parallel activity in the world of entertainment and in night life. Fashions change like the direction of the wind, but birds of a feather flock together, the renown of the one attracting the ambition of the other. And no one can really explain the strange meteorology which causes these seasonal changes nor foretell how long they will last!

Here, past history is inscribed less in the sites and the monuments than in books, in paintings or in prints. In these, humans replace stones but, more fragile than stone, they have left for us today only their shadows.

Here all places are meeting places. The churches and castles are cafés and even pleasure gardens and dance halls where several generations have burned out their evanescent youth.

What remains of so many joys that hid so much misery?—glories and reputations which have faded with the years. From the Moulin Rouge to the Bullier dance hall, from the Château des Brouillards to the Ruche, from Aristide Bruant to Henri Rousseau—known as douanier Rousseau because he had been a customs officer—from Toulouse-Lautrec to Modigliani, from Carco to Apollinaire, from Montmartre to Montparnasse, one meets only ghosts. But their works live on, less ephemeral than the victories of princes.

Montmartre is a village. But it is also a world, a most heterogeneous one at that! From the little Poulbots (urchins)—the children who inherited the name of the artist who created them, Poulbot—to the art students of uncertain talent, from impecunious recluses to the prostitutes of Pigalle, from poets to young loafers and from song writers to vagrants, a whole world lives on the Butte. Some of them live on illusions, others by their wits, but all are equally attached to this village which proclaimed itself a 'free commune' with its own mayor, band and firemen. This charming masquerade is reflected during the summer months in picturesque parades for the pleasure of lovers of folklore and the delight of tourists.

But for the tourist Montmartre means first and foremost, the Basilica of Sacré-Cœur whose whitish dome, on the highest point of the Butte, is seen on the

Below: view of the lake in the Bois de Boulogne. Right: modern buildings at the Porte Maillot which leads to the residential city of Neuilly and the Bois de Boulogne.

The impressive structures of the Paris of tomorrow: the area known as La Défense and the express metro line which, crossing the capital from east to west, links it to a number of outlying districts.

horizon from all corners of Paris.

Of Romano-Byzantine inspiration and heavily embellished like a 'set piece', Sacré-Cœur is nonetheless part of the Parisian landscape. The terraces and gardens, havens for the tired tourist, overlook the great city below and the mass of roofs and spires which throng the landscape as far as the eye can see.

Close by, the village steeple of a small church rises modestly. Saint-Pierre-de-Montmartre is one of the oldest churches in Paris. Consecrated in 1147 by Pope Eugene III, it was reconstructed during the ensuing centuries, but the choir, the apse and part of the nave date from the 12th century.

Saint-Pierre, all that remains of the Benedictine Abbey of Montmartre, is worthy of the village whose church it was for a long time. A representation of the Crucifixion in the church garden and the old Merovingian cemetery accentuate the site's archaic character.

Place du Tertre is the village square. In the summer above all, it is taken over by outdoor restaurants, where local daubers sit side by side in serried ranks. The outré people and "chromo-lithographers", naive painters and futurists, while-you-wait portraitists, they have more onlookers than clients but the Place du Tertre is their studio and their refuge. In the evening one dines under the Chinese lanterns. Round about, the restaurants advertise their centuries-old specialities and variety singers do their turns. Today's establishments were the pleasure gardens and inns of yesterday. All around the square the little streets live on their memories. At the corner of the Rue Saint-Rustique, the oldest street in Montmartre, the signboard 'A la bonne franquette' (without ceremony) has replaced that of the pleasure garden frequented by artists at the end of the last century. It was there that Van Gogh painted the picture (now in the Jeu de Paume museum) called *La Guinguette.*

At the corner of the Rue des Saules, the little house of the *Lapin Agile* (nimble rabbit)—which started life as the *Lapin à Gill* (Gill's rabbit)—has retained the rural look it had in Courtline's time. Later on, Apollinaire, Max Jacob and Francis Carco went there, and countless others.

Very close by, on the side of the hill lies the little acre of vines that is harvested each year with great Montmartrian pomp. There is a history attached to Montmartre's wine. It was appreciated by the Romans even before Julian's arrival. A certain Catilius Severus

praised its merits in his story of a trip he made to Lutetia about the year 305. "It is the wealth of the country," he wrote. "The Parisians curse the memory of the wicked Domitian who had all the vines pulled up, and bless good Probus who allowed them to be replanted."

In the 12th century, at a congress, the wine Goutte-d'Or (Drop of Gold), whose name was given to a Montmartre street, was adjudged to be one of the

best vintages. At that time there were vines almost everywhere on the Butte and also at Passy, Auteuil, Grenelle, and on Mont Sainte-Geneviève.

Little by little, to make way for buildings, the vines of Montmartre disappeared. In 1933 it was decided to plant 2000 vineplants from the Treille du Roy vineyards at Thoméry near Fontainebleau, in order to maintain the tradition and at the same time preserve the site. There are other vines to be found in Paris—e.g. at the Institute, the Palais-Bourbon, and in the Rohan courtyard, but it is the vines of Montmartre that symbolize today the renown of Paris wines.

Here, we are in the heart of old Montmartre. The praises of the Rue Saint-Vincent were sung by Aristide Bruant, who was the great draw at the *Chat-Noir*

A whole book could be made up solely of the picturesque signs of old Paris. Some specimens are shown on these two pages.

or Black Cat nightclub. Hector Berlioz lived in this same street and Paul Verlaine in the Rue Nicolet, not far from there.

But Montmartre's most famous and reputedly oldest house is located at 12 Rue Cortot. It was built by Rose de Rosimond, the actor who succeeded Molière, and down the centuries it has housed many illustrious tenants. Circa 1875 Auguste Renoir had his studio at 12 Rue Cortot, and it was there that he painted the *Moulin de la Galette.* Emile Bernard lived there and had as his neighbor the famous Christian polemicist, Leon Bloy. Suzanne Valadon lived there with her son Maurice Utrillo and her lover. Raoul Dufy had his studio there, and later passed it on to Othon Friesz. It was there that Poulbot created his 'Montmartre youngsters'.

Bits of the old house were restored after its acquisition by the city of Paris. The porch opens onto the courtyard onto which the studios look out, and a garden at the back is next to Montmartre's vineyard. Since 1960 the house has been the Museum of Old Montmartre.

From the top of the Butte, Rue Lepic goes down to the boulevards. It follows the line of a ridge on which, from the 17th to the beginning of the 19th century, stood the windmills, the charm of Montmartre. According to the French playwright Regnard, who wrote about them in the late 17th century, there were

The flea market at St-Ouen is, like that of London, among the most famous in the world. It has several sections selling furniture and knick-knacks which are unlike anything to be found anywhere else.

thirty of these windmills. By the 19th century there were no more than fifteen which were used to grind corn and press grapes. But already the far-seeing millers had been turning them into places of pleasure. "From the Cour aux Anes" (Donkeys' Courtyard), writes Jacques Hillairet," one went by donkey to the top of the Butte going up the steep climb which must have been the *Vieux Chemin* (Rue Ravignan). The site was charming, the panorama pleasant, and the miller's wife charming. She made good round griddle-cakes. The miller, an obliging man, kept in readiness a small orchestra of fifes, violins and oboes. One played, danced, dined and drank, and in the evening more than one cap was flung over the windmills."

The last pleasure windmill was the Moulin de la Galette, a famous dance hall of the Belle Epoque, whose familiar silhouette could still be seen at the corner of Rue Girardon 20 years ago. Now without its sails, it houses a small theater. But the mill of 20 years ago was not the original one but only a reconstruction undertaken in 1928. The only authentic survivor, is the Blute-Fin mill, inside the former "Jardin de Montmartre". It still has its sails and the little upper platform shown in Van Gogh's paintings.

It was in fact in Rue Lepic (No. 54) that Van Gogh lived for two years (1887-1888) in his brother Theo's home. The painter Guillaumin also lived in the house.

The Rue Girardon, which is at the corner of the Moulin de la Galette, leads—right after a recently laid-out public garden—to what was the 'Château des Brouillards', (Castle of Mists), a group of rather elegant buildings, the remains of a 'folly' constructed in the 18th century by the Marquis de Pompignan. Gérard de Nerval lived there in 1846. Then small pavilions were built in the former park. Auguste Renoir went to live in one of them at the end of the last century.

Opposite, the picturesque Rue d'Orchampt leads to the Place Emile-Gaudeau where the 'Bateau-Lavoir' was located. Neither boat nor washhouse, it was a group of irregular buildings, where cubism was born. Among the painters who lived there at the beginning of this century were Pablo Picasso, Kees van Dongen, Juan Gris, and among the poets Max Jacob, André Salmon, Pierre Mac-Orlan, as well as many of their friends who were more or less short-lived guests, from the art dealer Bing.

From the Rue des Abbesses, where the 'Dames de Montmartre' had their convent, several little streets lead down to the Boulevards Clichy and de Roche-chouart, until recently still called outer boulevards.

Quite another Montmartre is to be found between Place Clichy and the Barbès intersection. Here the post-Impressionists reigned at the end of the last century. Van Gogh called it the 'Petit Boulevard' as

Top left: the impressive tower of the ancient Château de Vincennes. Bottom: view of the Bois de Vincennes which, in the east of Paris, is as famous as its counterpart in the west, the Bois de Boulogne. Above: an old house typical of the valley of the Chevreuse, south of Paris.

opposed to the Grands Boulevards where the well-known Impressionists had their exhibitions. There already were numerous public establishments on Boulevard de Clichy and Place Blanche: restaurants and dance halls such as the Reine Blanche which had to give way in 1889 to the Moulin-Rouge, opened by the celebrated Zidler. He was to deprive the Elysée-Montmartre, another famous dance hall, on the Boulevard Rochechouart, of its stars, La Goulue and Valentin, the acrobat. Toulouse-Lautrec was the excellent portraitist of these two performers. His life as artist was spent either in the boulevard's music halls or the local brothels. Van Gogh and his friends exhibited their paintings at the 'Tambourin', run by an Italian woman, la Segatori. The café disappeared, to make way for the Quat'z Arts dance hall. But most of these cabarets which attracted a whole generation no longer exist: the Chat-Noir, where Aristide Bruant performed with great success, the Néant (nothingness), the Lune Rousse (red moon), and the Ciel and Enfer (Heaven and Hell) which faced each other. The greater part of the Boulevard de Clichy was reconstructed at the beginning of our century, and the music halls were replaced by cinemas and some theaters starring chansonniers (song-writers who sing their own compositions, normally consisting of pertinent comment on events or personages).

This area has, however, known tragic hours. It was here that, in March 1814 under Marshal Moncey, the National Guard, defended against the Cossacks the last gateway into Paris. His statue is on the

square. Today the outer boulevards and especially Place Blanche and Place Pigalle are the center for the lighter side of Montmartre's life. Cafés, restaurants, nightclubs line the sidewalks where the streetwalkers are on the job around the clock! The walls of the music halls are dominated by the pictures of nudes and in the dance halls the hostesses do everything to increase the bill. Behind this picturesque and special 'breed' lives another, less visible one, that of the Parisian underworld.

Beyond the boulevards is the Paris of business. But the Rue des Martyrs also had its famous cafés. Baudelaire, Jules Vallès, Banville often went to the Restaurant des Martyrs. The Nouvelle-Athènes was the meeting place of the post-Impressionists who were called the Manet 'gang', from Pissarro to Degas and Gauguin. The 'Divan Japonais' had its hour of glory at the time the singer Yvette Guilbert was drawing all Paris to hear her there. Then, at the beginning of this century, the face of Montmartre began to change. The artists were already starting their trek to Montparnasse.

Montparnasse is an intersection that the boulevard crosses like a river. Several « tributaries » flow into the main stream there, each bearing on the incoming tide its nocturnal pleasures and artistic ambitions.

There was no Boulevard du Montparnasse before the end of the 18th century and until the middle of the 19th century it still had a rural atmosphere. Pleasure gardens were laid out and a country-style dance hall, the Grande-Chaumière (thatched cottage), did a thriving trade with its gardens, grottoes, swings and even scenic railways. It is said that the polka first saw the light of day there, as well as the Cancan and the Rag, two dances 'daring' enough to be forbidden by the police.

The Grande-Chaumière disappeared in 1855. Little by little the boulevards built up. Several 18th century buildings have survived but the arrival of artists and political exiles in the second half of the 19th century, when a wind of freedom was blowing across Europe, was to determine the general character of Montparnasse in the years to come, making it unusually cosmopolitan.

The 'colonies' of 'advanced' minds whose ambition it was to renew art and society gathered in several cafés situated around the intersection of the Boulevard du Montparnasse and the Boulevard Raspail. Lenin and Trotsky patronized the Dôme, Picasso, Vlaminck, Modigliani the Rotonde, and other painters met in the Coupole. They attended the nearby schools of art. The Rue de la Grande-Chaumière with its studios and its shops that sell art supplies, still clings to its artistic vocation. A particular feature of this street is the old Colarossi Art School, now called the Charpentier, where Gauguin followed his friends Schuffenecker and Monfried. In 1917, Modigliani, who was then living in the Rue de la Grande-Chaumière, met Jeanne Hébuterne at this Art School.

Other impecunious artists found refuge in the neighboring quarter of Vaugirard at the Cité Falguière— which still has some studios, the most notable being the 'Ruche', the 'Bateau-Lavoir' of the left bank.

At the end of the Boulevard du Montparnasse a modernized café-restaurant, La Closerie des Lilas, also has its memories of great men. This was the meeting place of many writers and poets: Gide, Jarry, Moréas, Séverine and Paul Fort, the 'prince of poets', as well as of artists such as Dalou and Harpignies.

Today, Montparnasse by night means above all nightclubs, discothèques and theaters on the Rue Bréa, the Rue de la Gaîté and in the small thoroughfares that radiate from the former Montparnasse railroad station. Some years ago, the station was replaced by the huge 56-story tower.

On January 1, 1860, in application of a decree of the Chamber of Deputies, the limits of Paris were extended to the fortified wall built 18 years earlier by Thiers to assure the capital's defense. At one fell swoop Paris was thus enlarged by 11 communes and a part of the land of 13 others which continued to exist and today form part of Greater Paris.

On the right bank nine communes were annexed: Montmartre, Passy, Auteuil, Les Batignolles-Monceau, La Chapelle-Saint-Denis, La Villette, Belleville, Charonne and Bercy. Grenelle and Vaugirard were the two communes annexed on the left bank.

Annexation made districts of these communes, but for all that they lost neither their character nor the particular qualities of their activities and their population. It can be said that even today, though more so before

the last war, they are very different from each other. Passy does not resemble Belleville, nor is Auteuil like Bercy. Neither the streets nor the people in them look the same. One quarter conceals bourgeois life, another is a bustling world of work. At La Villette the talk is of meat, at Bercy it is of famous wines.

The history of the Paris communes is not so eventful as that of the heart of the capital, and their monuments in particular are not such as to attract the tourist's attention. But is that sufficient reason to ignore them ? To do so would be to deprive Paris of part of its charm and to underrate the humble folk who live in these districts. They too are attached to their habits and traditions, and it is because of this that the communes of Paris also had their poets and song writers. Wherever he sang throughout the world, Maurice Chevalier was the voice of Ménilmontant.

Until recently, Montmartre (to which reference has already been made), Belleville, Charonne and Bercy had retained their provincial air. Now they are losing it a little each day, as there rise in the sky of Paris the

The airport of Roissy-Charles-de-Gaulle, built on a plain north of Paris, is famous for the advanced nature of its design and architecture.

buildings and towers that relieve the congestion purify the air, standardize and disfigure. Would 'Maurice' recognize his neighborhood today?

Here and there old hovels collapse, "unhealthy spots" disappear. No one should regret their passing simply 'for love of the picturesque, but one can regret that the imagination of architects all over the world is so strangely uniform and that today a house in Paris resembles a house in Milan or San Francisco. It might be claimed that it is not the decree of 1860 which annexed the Paris communes, but modern town planning!

From Place Villiers to Place Wagram and Place Pereire, buildings in neo-Gothic, Second Empire and late 19th century styles are paramount. Many personalities in the world of the arts and literature fell victim to the taste for grandiose historic buildings. This was even more true of actors, to whom it no doubt gave the illusion of living in an operatic setting. The younger Coquelin lived on the Boulevard Malesherbes, as did Pierre Louÿs, Catulle Mendès, and Paul Déroulède and his rivals in patriotic painting, Meissonier and Detaille.

The Rue de Courcelles was the realm of the 'aristocratic world' whose decline was described by Marcel Proust, who himself lived there until his mother's death. The Duchess of Uzès, Prince Bibesco, the Queen-Mother of Spain, Princess Mathilda and Prince Cantacuzène were other inhabitants of the Rue de Courcelles. For Europe's nobility all roads led here.

Earlier, at the end of the 18th century Louis-Philippe of Orléans, Duke of Chartres, became interested in the village of Monceau. About 1780, he had the 'Folly of Chartres' built there, with a park that included a 'world of fantasy'. In it were Greek temples, Chinese pagodas, a Tatar tent, pyramids, obelisks, kiosks and mills, play-grounds and swings. What remains of this Folly, which was confiscated at the time of the Revolution and reduced in size by building development, is now the Parc Monceau. Some ancient trees have survived as well as the 'naumachia' ornamental lake decorated with a Corinthian colonnade. There is also a Renaissance archway which was brought from the Town Hall after the latter was burned down in 1871.

The Parc Monceau is an oasis of greenery in the very heart of Paris. Beyond to the east begins the district called Europe, which extends as far as St-Lazare station.

The Place de l'Etoile and the Avenue de la Grande-Armée separate the 17th arrondissement from the 16th. The latter, between the Seine and the Bois de Boulogne, includes the former villages of Passy, Auteuil and Chaillot. In the past they abounded in castles and the 'follies' that it was the pleasure of the great to build in the country.

Towards the middle of the 17th century, the discovery of the healing properties of the waters of Passy helped make the village well-known, but its fame as a thermal station was very ephemeral, despite an ambitious comparison with Forges and Spa. The Rue des Eaux (waters) is the only reminder of those days. The waters disappeared during the urbanization of Passy.

Nevertheless, Passy and Auteuil have remained the

fashionable sections of the capital. But the 'follies' have disappeared, to make way for the plutocratic buildings of the Belle Epoque which are so popular today with the French upper middle class.

To the north, leading off the Place de l'Etoile is Avenue Foch, the broadest avenue in Paris. It was built on the plans of Haussmann under the Second Empire. It is 390 feet wide, has stretches of grass and tree-lined walks. If the avenue could talk, it would tell of the fine horse-drawn carriages making their way last century to the Bois de Boulogne where they drove round the lake, less to give the horses exercise than to show off the occupants' wealth.

Here and there in Passy and Auteuil there still remain some vestiges of the past. The novelist Balzac's house, giving on to both Rue Reynouard and Rue Berton has become a museum of souvenirs in a setting of green. The garden opens into the Rue Berton, one of the narrowest in Paris. It measures just over five feet and a stream runs down the middle!

Other buildings of interest are the Clemenceau museum where the 'Tiger' lived for 34 years, the Marmottan museum, rich in works by Monet, and the Radio and TV building in front of the Seine, a successful and rather beautiful example of modern architecture. Built in 1963, it has more than 1,000 offices, 70 recording studios and a tower almost 230 feet high.

Opposite, the Ile des Cygnes (Isle of Swans), consisting of a long promenade lined with trees, is a peaceful place insufficiently known by Parisians themselves.

The Bois de Boulogne is the vastest forest in Paris. With its lakes, its zoo, its floral park of Bagatelle, the Bois is very popular with those who like walking, horse-riding and canoeing. Although many very busy roads pass through the wood, the pedestrian has plenty of charming walks to choose from, especially in the central part—at least until the end of the day. At night, it is forbidden for pedestrians to go there and for cars to park but it is nevertheless the refuge of a very special type of human fauna. 'Honest people' are recommended to avoid it at night.

Beyond the Fermiers-Généraux wall and to the east of Montmartre, the suburban communes spread over a zone that is bounded by the outer boulevards that continue those of the west—the Boulevards La Chapelle, La Villette, de Belleville, de Ménilmontant, de Charonne and de Picpus.

Like a cup that is full to overflowing, Paris spills over into its periphery. Successive walls enlarged the city's territory without greatly modifying its form, and 'Greater Paris' continues to spread in concentric zones. Of the gates that marked the city's limits, only the names remain. They are now intersections by which the hordes of workers return home every evening.

This development followed the same pattern of that of the communes of Paris and, curiously enough, a glance at a map of the city, shows that, on the outskirts and at the center alike, the aristocrats are on the left side and the plebs on the right!

St-Cloud and St-Germain are extensions of Auteuil and Passy, as Romainville and Créteil are of Belleville

Left: view of the Parc de Sceaux. Below: the Château de Fontainebleau.

To the west of Paris, Versailles, a symbol of the greatness of France's past. Above, left: the ceremonial gateway at the entrance to the château and a general view. Lower left : view of the park of Versailles with the famous pool by Latone; note the perspective offered by the receding ponds across the grounds of the palace. Right: a promenade in the park at Versailles.

Versailles: above, a view of the Grand Trianon. Below: the 'Hameau' of Queen Marie-Antoinette. Right: view of the Petit Trianon.

and Charonne; the reason lies in modern demography.

But, in past centuries the belt around Paris was a royal crown, whose jewels were those marvelous estates that still delight us today: Versailles, St-Germain, Marly-le-Roi, St-Cloud, Sceaux.

Castles and parks, hills and forests, the green belt of Paris evokes the image of another age. The carriages rolled over royal roads and the Parisians of the 'Grand Siècle' built their 'follies' at the edge of woods or on hillsides.

As it leaves Paris behind, the Seine describes a wide bend, as if delaying its progress in sad farewell. Again and again, between Suresnes and Chatou and from Chatou to Maisons-Laffitte it winds its way onwards, clearly reluctant to abandon the city.

To the north of Paris, the Porte de Clignancourt is the shore on which the flotsam is washed up for the joy of the buyers. This vast 'bargain' counter is called the 'flea-market'—although that biting insect is not necessarily a part of the goods that buyers fight over. The strangest objects are found there, utensils from another age but sometimes also valuable antiques and collector's treasures!

Beyond, the avenues converge on St-Denis where, according to legend, the missionary saint of Lutetia arrived, carrying his decapitated head in his hands.

A splendid basilica recalls his martyr. Begun in 1122 on the initiative of Louis VII's Minister, the Abbé Suger, this was the first important building of Gothic art. Under Saint Louis, the work was taken up again, and down the centuries the basilica was the burial place of the kings of France. The tombs, with their effigies of recumbent figures, still in the large nave, are empty, the ashes having been scattered to the winds by the revolutionaries of 1789.

It was rightly said that the Saint-Denis Basilica was the richest museum of French funerary sculpture from the Middle Ages to the Renaissance."

In the 18th century the buildings of the former abbey were reconstructed under the direction of Jacques-Ange Gabriel. In 1809 Napoléon set up there an educational establishment of the Legion of Honor. It is a very beautiful complex with the cloister, the chapter house, the dining hall, the monumental staircases and the 67 acre park surrounding the buildings.

Above all, Vincennes calls to mind the legendary image of Saint Louis dispensing justice under an oak tree. For several centuries the castle was the favorite residence of the kings of France. Although it was constantly being enlarged and renovated until the reign of Louis XIV, who had Le Vau build a King's Pavilion and a Queen's Pavilion, it was under the Valois dynasty that the castle of Vincennes enjoyed its most brilliant hours.

Big hunting parties were given at Vincennes, Louis XIV lived there at the beginning of his marriage with Maria Theresa, and fell in love with Louise de La Vallière during a party at the castle.

The dungeon was also a prison which held famous inmates: Henry of Navarre, who later became Henri IV, Fouquet, Diderot, the celebrated adventurer Latude, Mirabeau and the Marquis de Sade.

Of the old buildings, only the imposing dungeon and the 16th century surrounding fortified wall now remain. The chapel of the same epoch was not finished until the 16th century.

Around the castle were the grounds of the royal hunt. The forest as it is today was the work, during the Second Empire, in the taste of the time, with lakes, streams and rock gardens. For the inhabitants of the nearby suburb this is a very popular place for a stroll.

To the south, the Bois de Vincennes extends to the shores of the Marne which, like the Seine, winds its way between the grassy banks.

Particularly since last century, the main feature of this part of the forest has been its pleasure gardens on the banks and the islands of the river. Nogent-sur-Marne, where Watteau died, Le Perreux and Joinville are centers of canoeing. In former times, restaurants, where fried fish was served, welcomed happy, noisy couples; some of these places are still in existence. The calm has returned in front of the pleasant houses which border the river. Parisians no longer go to the suburbs, preferring to race along the roads for a weekend in the provinces. And the suburbanites go to Paris! "But where are the oarsmen of yesteryear?"

A little to the south of the Marne is the State-owned 17th century castle of Champs. Madame de Pompadour lived at Champs, where two of her distinguished visitors were Louis XV and Voltaire.

The crown of Paris has its diamond—Versailles. Have Royal power and its magnificence ever been expressed with such brilliance?

In the beginning Versailles was no more than a lodge, built by Louis XIII on the land where he loved to hunt. Louis XIV went there as a child and, after his marriage, decided to construct the palace of his dreams as a monument to his own greatness.

Four centuries of French history are enshrined within these walls. Some of France's most glorious and most dramatic hours have struck here. Versailles was the scene of the "Sun King's" most sumptuous display, and it was there that the States General assembled on the eve of the Revolution. It was at Versailles that the arrival of the Parisian mob, come to seize the royal family, marked the downfall of the monarchy. It was in the Hall of Mirrors that the Germans proclaimed their Empire in 1871 after the French defeat. Forty years later, on June 29, 1919, in that selfsame Versailles, another peace was signed, confirming the allied victory over Germany.

From Louis XIV to the present day works of art have been accumulated in the castle, which became a museum under the Republic. Paintings, sculpture, ornamentation, jewelry, furniture, all that artists could produce to glorify their princes and extol their conquests is laid out there, a fabulous exuberance of riches.

The royal apartments, the salons of state, the guardrooms, the Hall of Mirrors, all merit a visit. From the terrace the park's descent is graduated, each level having its fountains and its statues. At the end of a wide avenue, known as the Green Carpet, is the Grand Canal.

Beyond the park is the Grand Trianon, a delightful building of white and rose marble with colonnades, which opens onto a terrace resplendent with flowers. The intimate and rustic charm of the Petit Trianon and especially the 'Hameau' in the gardens, is enchanting, coming as it does after the austere grandeur of the castle. The 'Hameau' was erected for Marie-Antoinette about 1775. There are some rare trees in the park to add to the charm of its ponds, its river, its paths and its mill. Through the water-lilies in the pond shimmers the reflection of the Temple of Love. The 'Hameau' makes one dream of the days when, so it is said, kings married shepherdesses.

A visit to some of the other estates is also rewarding, as much for the interest of their historic souvenirs as for the beauty of their surroundings. Autoroutes and railways put these 'satellites' of its glory within a few minutes' distance of Paris.

A visit to Paris and its environs should include the castle of Malmaison, and that of Bois-Bréau, which completes it. Here at Malmaison the memory of Napoleon and Josephine de Beauharnais, who died there in 1814, still lives. It was from Malmaison that, in 1815, the Emperor took the road to exile. Though modest by comparison with Versailles, the residence is charming and rich in relics of the Emperor and his Empire.

Royal souvenirs are also to be found in the castle of St.-Germain-en-Laye which was originally a country-seat built for King Robert next to the abbey founded in 1010.

Philip-Augustus, Saint Louis, Charles V, all three made a fortified castle of this residence. Francis I transformed it into a palace and had a park laid out. Here, he and the beautiful Diane de Poitiers assembled around them a brilliant Court. Henry IV and Marie de Medici, often stayed at St.-Germain. Louis XIV was born there and Louis XII died there, as did James II, the dethroned king of England.

Louis XIV offered the residence to Louise de la Vallières when he left her for Madame de Montespan, but it was not enough to console her.

Le Nôtre finished the magnificent terrace begun under Henry II. Then the castle ceased to find favor in royal eyes. During the Revolution it served as a barracks, it became a cavalry school under the Empire, and a prison under Louis-Philippe. Napoleon III restored it, for use as a museum of National Antiques.

The position of St.-Germain, and its lovely Renaissance decoration and the chapel of Saint Louis, hold the visitor's attention as much as the terrace invites him to take a stroll on the promenade. Overlooking the Seine, it extends for more than a mile and offers very beautiful views over the towns and the greenery, as far as to Paris.

Right: the Château de la Malmaison; bottom: entrance to the royal château of Saint-Germain-en-Laye.